GRATITUDE

A positive new approach to raising thankful kids

Dannielle Miller, B.Ed.

with Vanessa Mickan

Inlumino
Sydney, Australia

Praise for *Gratitude*

"Dannielle Miller has a uniquely insightful way of exploring key issues around parenting that concern us all. In her latest book she explores the increasing modern phenomenon of increasing ingratitude and narcissism and how this self-centered perception of the world can impact negatively on our mental, emotional, and social wellbeing—especially for our children. Thanks, Danni, for being such a positive champion and guide for parents and teachers to help them build gratitude and thoughtfulness in our children so that we can create a more caring and compassionate world for all."

Maggie Dent, parenting and resilience educator, and author of *Nurturing Kids' Hearts and Souls* and *Saving Our Adolescents*

"With so many parents worried they're raising a generation of entitled, ungrateful kids, Dannielle Miller's book Gratitude is the antidote. It's a must-have for every parent's bookshelf."

Rebecca Sparrow, columnist, author, and speaker

"Written in such warm, engaging, and accessible prose, and drawing on her vast personal and professional experiences as well as the advice of other experts, Dannielle Miller has created a gem of a book. An invaluable resource for parents, teachers, and anyone looking to rebuild balance and meaning in their lives and those of their children, Gratitude explores the ways in which adults can build a sense of appreciation and thoughtfulness in younger generations. How, through the simple act of thankfulness we can restore empathy and kindness to lives that sometimes seem devoid of both. Gratitude reminds us that while we're individuals, we're also part of a community, and it's by nurturing and modeling relationships that are compassionate, family, and community-focused, we all thrive."

Dr Karen Brooks, Author, and Associate Professor and Honorary Senior Research Fellow, Centre for Critical and Cultural Studies, University of Queensland

Published by Inlumino Enterprises Pty Ltd

Sydney, Australia

www.danniellemiller.com

First published by Inlumino Enterprises in 2014

ISBN 978-0-9941856-1-7

Cover image by istockphoto.com.au

Cover design by Rachel Ainge

Printed by Tien Wah Press

Contents

Introduction

One Christmas Day, I logged on to Facebook to wish my online friends all my love. I am frequently contacted by bright and amazing young women who were inspired and moved by my girl-empowering workshops, and it's a source of joy to me that we often stay connected, including on Facebook. But on this day, I was immediately struck by how many of the teen girls in my online world were listing off their Christmas gift haul, with no mention of the family or friends who had given them the gifts, and no sense of thankfulness. Others were outright complaining about their gifts—for example, "Hate my life. Got the black iPhone not the white." (Talk about a first-world problem!) Many whined that Christmas "sucked" or was "so boring."

I'm the mother of two smart, funny, big-hearted, and thoughtful children—a daughter, Teyah, who was 13 years old then, and a son, Kye, who was 11. Even they seemed to think that Christmas was falling short. There had been grumbles about the standard of the gifts they'd received and about the fact that the holiday had never been the same since their father and I had divorced.

The post I wrote on my timeline turned out to be a lot different to the simple holiday greeting I'd sat down to write:

It's made me sad to see a number of my teen friends whining on here that Christmas feels lame now they're older. I've heard similar things at home too. You know what? You only get out what you put in to Christmas (and life). If you just sit back and do the gift inventory of everything you're getting, then yep, now that there's no magical Santa element, it may feel all a bit flat. Once you move past the little kid stage, the only way to really FEEL the Season is to be Loving! Kind! Grateful! And try not to fall into the trap of doing the "Family Inventory" either i.e: because we don't have a big family, we are not a "real" family; or because our mother is single, we are not "normal." Families come in all shapes and sizes. Sometimes, as we get older, we even invent our own through our friendships.

So how about this. Get off Facebook and hang with YOUR family – in whatever form it is in, at this point in time.

And try saying thank you – with heart. :)

My post attracted 117 likes in an hour and some of the most animated comments from parents and teens I've ever had on my timeline. The general consensus from parents—and the confession from teens—was that young people are not always very good at saying thank you or feeling grateful.

That Christmas Day was the catalyst for this book. Knowing that as a parent I was not alone in my concerns, I wanted to find out why gratitude matters and what we can do to help our children develop it. I began to look into it, and I soon learned that gratitude is such a vital part of being human that the field is a hotbed of research among psychologists.

As every parent knows, surly ingratitude from kids can make life miserable, but nurturing a grateful attitude is about so much more than simply making our days more pleasant or turning our kids into etiquette experts. There is plenty of solid evidence that encouraging a grateful attitude in our kids isn't just a nice thing to do, it's valuable parenting work because it sets children up with important skills for life.

According to one study from 2012, grateful teens are happier, better behaved at school, and more hopeful than their less-grateful peers. The most grateful teens have the highest life satisfaction, are more likely to believe that their life has meaning, have fewer symptoms of depression, and are less likely to cheat at school, take drugs, and drink alcohol.

And cultivating gratitude is good not only for the happiness of your own children, it's good for everybody, according to the researcher who conducted the study, Giacomo Bono, a psychology professor at California State University. In his words, "more gratitude may be precisely what our society needs to raise a generation that is ready to make a difference in the world."

I am passionate about empowering children to become the happiest, most fulfilled adults they have the potential to be. That is why I've devoted my life to working as an educator, running workshops to help children and their parents navigate the teen years, and writing parenting and teen advice books. But rest assured this isn't one of those parenting books where you will feel pressured to be the "perfect" parent. I am not about to proclaim myself the expert who has all the answers to raising grateful children. I wrote this book as a parent exploring the best ways to nurture gratitude in kids—and in myself, too. What I learned along the way has not only helped me to encourage my children to have a more grateful attitude, it has deepened my own appreciation for all that I have in my life.

One thing I learned is that there is no magical formula for transforming children from whining that they got the wrong color iPhone into paragons of gratitude. (If only!) There can be no one single right way to teach gratitude to children, because every child and every family is unique. But there are so many fantastic ideas for encouraging children to be more grateful that I am sure some of the tips in this book will resonate with you and your children.

Looking at the books about gratitude that were already out there, I felt that plenty offered gratitude practices within a Christian framework. For some readers gratitude will be centered around thankfulness to God, but I know that for other readers gratitude may spring from different sources. So the tips and discussions you will find in this book are open and accessible to everyone, regardless of religious or spiritual beliefs. I think that gratitude and kindness are ethical choices that can transcend religious and cultural differences and strengthen the bonds between us all.

The advice, wisdom, and practical ideas you will find here come from my experiences as a parent, as an educator, and from working with thousands of young men and women. It comes from experts such as psychologists. And it comes from the ultimate experts: the legion of other parents who came before us and learned at their dining tables, during birthday parties, on long car trips, and while tucking their kids into bed what the best ways are to raise grateful children.

I brought my friend and longtime editor, Vanessa Mickan, on board to help out with this project. With Vanessa based on the east coast of the United States and me in Sydney, Australia, we have been able to draw on a wide range of perspectives on gratitude.

We've both tried and tested a number of gratitude practices—and we can tell you, this stuff works!

I hope you find ideas that work for you and help you bring a deeper, richer sense of gratitude, abundance, and joy into your family's life. Thank you for reading, and thank you for sharing my passion to nurture gratitude in our children.

Dannielle Miller

Why gratitude is so important

A thankful heart is a happy heart

In recent years there has been a big growth spurt in the field of positive psychology. It is a discipline that extends psychology beyond the treatment of psychological problems and focuses on helping people to actively thrive. Essentially, it's the science of how to be happier and have a more positive outlook on life. And when it comes to the research on what drives happiness and a healthy mental attitude, the stand-out is gratitude.

Martin Seligman, known as the father of positive psychology, took a group of people who described themselves as seriously depressed and asked them to spend a few moments each day for 15 days writing down three good things that happened to them that day. The results were nothing short of amazing for such a quick and simple practice: 94% said their depression had eased, and 92% said they were happier. What we focus our attention on has an incredibly powerful effect on our feelings and actions.

Two psychologists who are prominent in the gratitude field, Robert Emmons and Michael McCullough, from University of California Davis, took one group of people and asked them to write down five things for which they were grateful, once a week for 10 weeks. A second group was asked to list five things that were a hassle or an annoyance. And, finally, a third group was asked to list five things that affected them, without emphasizing either the good or the bad aspects. At the end of the 10 weeks, the people who were asked to write down what they were grateful for were 25% happier than the other groups. There were even physical benefits: the gratitude group had fewer health complaints and exercised more than the others. In fact, they exercised almost 1.5 hours more each week than those who dwelled on their annoyances.

Emmons and McCullough went on to do a similar study, but this time the three groups of people were asked to write down their reflections each day for three weeks. That timing turned out to be key, increasing gratitude even more than the weekly practice. The list of benefits that the people in the gratitude group experienced reads like a catalogue of awesome that we would all wish for our kids (and ourselves). The gratitude group felt "more joyful, enthusiastic, interested, attentive, energetic, excited, determined, and strong" than the people who wrote down their hassles once a day. They slept better, too, falling asleep quicker, getting more hours of sleep each night, and waking more refreshed. And the researchers found that cultivating an attitude of gratefulness changed people's behavior. The gratitude group reported giving other people more support and help with personal problems, and the truth of this was confirmed when people who knew the participants were surveyed.

It is proven that children as well as adults get a big happiness boost from cultivating gratitude. When schoolchildren in 6th and 7th grade were asked to list either five things they were grateful for or five hassles every day for two weeks, the ones who focused on gratitude ended up with a more positive outlook about school and greater life satisfaction. When psychologists analyzed parents' descriptions of their children's strengths, they found that the more grateful children were, the more satisfied they were with life. In another study, high school students who showed high levels of gratitude were found to have better academic performance, less depression and envy, and a more positive attitude to life than their less grateful peers.

We all want happy, positive kids—that's a no-brainer. But just in case anyone out there is thinking, "That's great, but show me the tangible benefits," research has found that a happy, positive outlook is the font from which springs many important lifelong skills and attributes. Would you like your children to be "more creative, helpful, charitable, and show greater self-regulatory and coping abilities"? These are all attributes of happy people. And happiness has been shown to lead to happy outcomes, such as greater productivity and success in the workplace, longer-lasting and more satisfying marriages, a wider circle of friends, a bigger support network, more energy, a stronger immune system, lower levels of stress, less physical pain, and a longer life. Cultivating happiness is serious business!

More gratitude, stronger relationships

If you can encourage your children to feel and show gratitude, their world will become a kinder, more supportive place in which to live. That's because another important benefit of practicing gratitude is that it strengthens empathy and the social bonds between people. Grateful people have been shown to be more likely to nurture their relationships and less likely to be lonely. Because they focus on all the things and people in their lives they have to be thankful for, they are more likely to feel loved and looked after, which strengthens their relationships.

But it's not just about subjectively feeling more loved and less lonely, for when we express gratitude to another person it often has the magical effect of causing that person to do something nice for us in return. The chain of thankfulness and generosity need never end—it's just up to us to keep it going. Failing to show gratitude— or worse, showing ingratitude—removes a link from the chain and almost guarantees that the other person will think twice about doing something nice for us in the future.

Researchers found that gratitude leads to greater social bonding when they studied teen girls who were joining sororities in the United States (social organizations for female undergraduate students). The new girls reported having the greatest levels of gratitude when older sorority sisters made them feel cared for, understood, and valued. What's interesting is that a girl's level of gratitude predicted how strongly she would feel connected to the other sorority members and the sorority as a whole. The more grateful a girl was, the stronger the connection.

Gratitude helps younger children create supportive networks, too. Grateful children aged 11–13, compared to their less-grateful peers, have better social support, give more emotional support to others, and are more satisfied with their social networks, such as their school, family, community, and friends. And grateful kids aged 14–19 are more likely to use their talents to better their community.

I believe that adopting a grateful attitude can even help to turn the wider world around you into part of your social network by enhancing your everyday interactions with people. Imagine you've got your hands full and a stranger holds a door open for you. "Thanks," you say, and you look the person in the eye and smile because you genuinely feel grateful that he or she took the time to hold the door open for you. Chances are, the person will smile back and you will feel a genuine friendly connection, even though you are under no obligation to be nice to each other. In that moment, you are reminded of the goodness in people. Now multiply that one little moment across all your interactions in any given day, and by the time your head hits the pillow for sleep, the world could be looking like a pretty great place to live. Gratitude is the glue that binds people together, while ingratitude makes us isolated and vulnerable. If you can help your children to genuinely feel grateful and show it, you will be helping them to create a positive, supportive world all around them, wherever they go, all throughout their life.

Gratitude may be protective

Early in my career as an educator, I assessed and advised on programs aimed at keeping students at school when they were at risk of dropping out. Then I went on to set up a program called the Lighthouse Project, to help at-risk students meet their full potential; it's still going strong and changing kids' lives. This field has remained a passion of mine, so I was really interested to see that researchers have turned their attention to the role gratitude can play in helping at-risk students. Psychologist Mindy Ma,

"Gratitude turns what we have into enough, and more. It turns denial into acceptance, chaos into order, confusion into clarity ... it makes sense of our past, brings peace for today, and creates a vision for tomorrow."

Melody Beattie

and her colleagues studied African-American children aged 12–14 in low-income, low-performing urban schools. They wanted to see if having a grateful attitude could help buffer these students from stress at home and at school.

First they surveyed almost 400 students to find out how grateful they felt toward people who did things that benefited them, and how much they focused on and appreciated the positive things in their lives. The researchers found that the children who felt grateful to people who did things to benefit them were more interested in their academic studies, in achieving good academic results, and in their extracurricular activities. The children who appreciated the positives in life were the least likely to take part in risky behaviors such as drug use and unsafe sex. Both types of gratitude—for people and for the positive things in life—were linked with positive family relationships.

The messages I take from this research are that a grateful attitude can have a concrete impact on a child's life, and that children need people in their lives who help to nurture an appreciation of all the good that exists in life, even in the midst of challenges.

A powerful motivator

I left working in the education system and started my own business, Enlighten Education, in 2003 with my friend and fellow educator Francesca. We've grown the company into a highly successful team of amazing women presenting workshops to thousands of teen girls every year. The business has become so well established that in recent times I've been able to branch out to provide workshops for boys. I put a lot of my business success down to the strength of the relationships I've built along the way. I believe that one of my most crucial roles as CEO is to acknowledge the brilliant workshop presenters who deliver our positive, affirming messages. I am genuinely thankful when my team do exceptional work. And I've witnessed the huge positive impact it has on them when I wholeheartedly express my gratitude.

Yet in the workplace it's often forgotten that gratitude is one of the biggest motivators. People are inspired to do their best work when they feel that their efforts are noticed and that their boss is grateful for what they do. For most people, monetary rewards are secondary to acknowledgment. In fact, failing to acknowledge a staff member's effort is "almost as bad as shredding their effort before their eyes," according to Dan Ariely, a professor of psychology and behavioral economics at Duke University. He did a study in which people were paid to find pairs of identical letters on a page full of random letters. They were divided into three groups. The first group wrote their names on their sheets before handing them in, and someone looked at each sheet and acknowledged each participant with an "Uh huh" before adding the sheet to a pile. The second group anonymously handed in their sheets, which were put in a pile without being looked at. The sheets of the people in the third group went straight into a paper shredder.

"Gratitude is the key to opening all doors."

Lailah Gifty Akita

All of the groups were asked to perform this task multiple times, and each time they were offered less money than the previous time. In order to keep doing the task, the people whose work was destroyed required *two times as much money* as the ones who were acknowledged. And the ones whose work was placed in a pile but left unacknowledged needed almost as much money as those whose work disappeared into the gaping maw of the shredder. That means benign neglect, which is the standard in many workplaces, can have just as corrosive an effect on motivation as negating someone's effort entirely.

The ability to acknowledge and thank staff is not something you wake up one day in your 30s knowing how to do. A grateful attitude and an understanding of the most effective ways to express gratitude need to be developed from a young age. One reason why it's so important that we foster gratitude in our kids is that these skills can really benefit them in their careers when they grow up.

I am inspired when I see entrepreneurship in children, because I know the freedom and sense of personal fulfilment that success in business can bring. And I know from my own experiences that gratitude plays a crucial role in building a business. I have been able to forge mutually beneficial, solid relationships that have boosted my business by acknowledging—in word and deed— those who have contributed to my achievements and successes. These include not only the people who make up my team but other professionals in my field who have informed and supported my work. I try to give back to them by helping to promote their work as well as my own and by finding ways to say thanks.

Smart companies know there is a benefit to giving thanks. One spectacular example of this was when TD Bank asked dozens of customers to branches in Canada on the pretense that they were going to help with market research about a new type of ATM. When they got there, they were surprised to find that the ATM spat out not cash but valuable thank-you gifts. One mother who said she'd never been able to afford to take her two sons anywhere on vacation received a family trip to Disneyland and money for their education. Another woman was flown to Trinidad to visit her daughter who was healing from cancer surgery. Of course, businesses don't do this sort of thing just out of the goodness of their hearts. They have entire departments and budgets set aside to reward customers, because they know their largesse will likely pay off.

The bank's promotion was especially effective because the gifts were personalized and meaningful, so the whole thing seemed sincere. In our daily lives, our shows of gratitude have to not just *appear* sincere; they have to come from a place of genuine thankfulness. And they have to be done without any expectation that we'll get something back in return. (You know that sinking feeling you get when you realize that someone's "Thank you" really means "What will you do for me now?")

Our gestures of thanks also don't have to be as expensive as, say, booking flights to Disneyland every time someone does something nice for us. Nor do they have to be complicated or time consuming. Showing gratitude can be as simple as sending a batch of cupcakes. I was utterly thrilled when I was named as a finalist in *InStyle* magazine's Women of Style Awards in the Charity and Community category, so the day before the awards presentation I sent cupcakes to the magazine's office. I included a letter thanking the staff and explaining how much it meant to me to be a finalist and how honored I was to be going to the award presentation. I had nothing to gain by doing this. After all, the judges had long since made their decision. It just felt important to me to take the time to thank people who had been supportive.

I was amazed how many of the *InStyle* staff came up to me on the night of the awards, quite teary, and said things like, "We were so touched. It's rare for someone to do something like that for us." I hope that when the current generation of children has grown up and entered the workplace, simple acts of gratitude like this will be commonplace.

Giving thanks and giving support to the people who have supported my business has not left me with less. Actually, it's brought more abundance to my business, and to my personal life, too.

Ingratitude is associated with:

anger	greed
resentment	bitterness
envy	shrinking sense of self

Gratitude is associated with:

joy	stronger social support
enthusiasm	richer social interactions
love	less loneliness
happiness	more energy
optimism	stronger immune system
forgiveness	
reduced depression	lower stress
reduced materialism	cardiovascular benefits
resilience in the face of trauma	less pain
	better sleep
greater number of friends	longer life

Why gratitude can be a challenge—for kids and parents

We do not enter this world grateful

Most children learn to say "please" and "thank you" at a fairly early age—though at first they usually need a tireless parent to continually prod, remind, and cajole them into it. The "thank yous" we receive from very small children may sound token or halfhearted, but there's a good reason for that: in order to feel true gratitude, our brains need to have developed to the point where we are able to recognize when someone has done something to benefit us and can appreciate the positive things in our lives. Children may begin to be able to say "thank you" without prompting between the ages of 4 and 6, but they still have a long way to go. They need to be taught—kindly and gently and gradually—how to be grateful, because just as language and other cognitive skills take time to develop, gratitude is a way of thinking that needs time to grow and be nurtured. What this means is that as we make an effort to cultivate gratitude in our families, we need to have a little (okay, maybe a lot!) of patience, especially

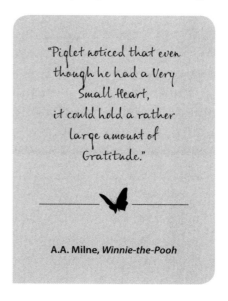

"Piglet noticed that even though he had a Very Small Heart, it could hold a rather large amount of Gratitude."

A.A. Milne, *Winnie-the-Pooh*

with children under the age of 7. By 12, children generally have the capacity to interpret situations and recognize when someone's actions warrant their gratitude.

We should lay the groundwork for gratitude as early as possible. Psychologists Jeffrey Froh and Giacomo Bono say that by showing a high level of warmth and empathy to children in their early years, while also setting firm boundaries, parents can help put their kids on a path toward gratitude. It also helps to have ongoing conversations with children about their own and other people's thoughts and feelings, because "children's comprehension of gratitude by age five is stronger if they have a better understanding of emotional and mental states."

A narcissistic world = a gratitude-free world

Instilling gratitude in children can sometimes feel like an uphill battle given they are growing up in a culture that increasingly seems to forgive narcissism, and even reward it if a quick glance at celebrity news websites and reality TV is anything to go by.

Narcissists have an inflated sense of self, are arrogant, and think they're unique and special. They believe they are entitled to be treated better than others, they take credit for others' achievements, and they struggle to form lasting relationships. Highly materialistic, continually seeking attention, and very vain about their appearance, they get angry or even violent when things don't go their way. The clincher, when it comes to gratitude, is that they lack warmth and empathy. In order to feel grateful to someone who has given us a gift or done something nice for us, we have to be able to put ourselves inside the heart and mind of the gift giver and understand his or her altruism. Without empathy, that just can't happen. Narcissists also have a strong sense of entitlement, so when they receive gifts, they don't see them as something for which they need to be thankful. They believe that whatever is given to them is theirs by right.

The number of people who can clinically be diagnosed with narcissistic personality disorder (NPD) is still small—only about 1 percent of the population—but that number is on the rise, at least in young people. Jean Twenge, a psychology professor at San Diego State University, who conducted a long-running study of 16,000 college students, said that while the average person is only moderately more narcissistic than a couple of decades ago, when it comes to clinical NPD, three times as many young people as older people now have the disorder. So you're not imagining that there are more highly narcissistic people around. Twenge believes that we can see the effect of this in our culture in the form of increased materialism, entitlement, public displays of violence and aggression, self-promotion, narcissistic song lyrics, plastic surgery, credit card debt, and the size of homes.

> "In normal life we hardly realize how much more we receive than we give, and life cannot be rich without such gratitude. It is so easy to overestimate the importance of our own achievements compared with what we owe to the help of others."

Dietrich Bonhoeffer

"Children today are growing up in a world that is much more accepting of narcissistic behavior and values," she says. "Many parents and teachers believe that the way to counteract this is to teach children to feel special. Unfortunately, feeling special is narcissism, not true self-worth."

According to Karen Brooks, associate professor at the University of Queensland Centre for Critical and Cultural Studies, we have created problems for kids by "handing out ribbons to every child in a race; discouraging competition, ensuring no report card contains words that might offend, upset, or indicate (God forbid) how ordinary or bad a child's performance at school really is."

Rather than helping kids to develop self-esteem, "what we are really doing is producing kids who are narcissistic because we focus too much on telling them how good they are, how wonderful they are, how everything they do is fantastic," says Deakin University Adjunct Professor Helen McGrath.

We need to concentrate on helping our children to build real self-esteem, rather than false self-esteem. Real self-esteem is not something we give to children by telling them they are special. It is something that grows in children as they develop skills and become more competent and confident. It is all about connectedness, compassion and community—an ability to empathize with others. And from that empathy, true gratitude can arise.

More means less: the abundance paradox

Anyone who's ever been on the receiving end of a child's ingratitude knows that one of the most infuriating things about it is their lack of awareness of just how good they've got it. The year I urged my young friends on Facebook to be more loving, kind, and grateful at Christmas, my then 13-year-old daughter was also complaining about the holiday, and it completely floored me. You see, she knew that the next day I was taking her to the USA for a couple of weeks of shopping, sightseeing, hilarity, and adventure. Flying all the way from Australia. We were even going to see the ball drop in Times Square on New Year's Eve! Oh, and as a special treat, I had splashed out on business-class tickets—you know, with flight attendants calling you by name, warm hand towels, yummy meals, and pajamas to wear in your fully reclining sleeping pod. Her life was super tough. Someone call Child Services! (My son, Kye, opted to stay in Sydney with his dad instead, because to him the idea of weeks of shopping and Broadway shows was hell—if he had to join us, he definitely would have called Child Services!)

While it is easy for us as adults to see how absurd it is to be grateful in the midst of plenty, imagine for a moment what it's like from our children's point of view. Compared to any previous time in history, children in the developed world are growing up with far more stuff to want, far more channels by which that stuff is marketed and advertised to them, and more disposable income or credit cards in our wallets with which to buy that stuff. Only a few generations ago, at Christmas a child might have been delighted to get a stocking filled with fruits, nuts, sweets, and trinkets. Compare that to the vast array of toys, electronics, music, shoes, makeup, clothes, and so on children are now convinced they *need*. Oxygen, water, food, shelter, love—these are what we really need. But thanks to sophisticated marketing and advertising, celebrity endorsements, and children's strong and valid urge to fit in, high-price consumer goods can seem essential to survival.

Even when children do receive the things they want, it doesn't necessarily make them happy, because they are living in a state called the "abundance paradox." Sociologist Christine Carter, of the Greater Good Science Center at the University of California, Berkeley, puts it this way: "Their disappointment when they don't get what they want is greater than their gratitude when they do get what they want." This is because gratitude comes much more easily in times of scarcity. Carter uses the example of a child growing up in a home where there isn't enough to eat. That child is likely to be more grateful and less picky about the food that is on his or her plate compared to a child whose fridge is full of goodies. Similarly, generations ago it would have been easier to please children with gifts because their closets weren't already stuffed to bursting with consumer goods. Carter notes that "even underprivileged children in the West have more than most children in the world, who live in developing nations."

As a parent of children who are fortunate to live in comfortable circumstances, I don't want to deprive them of the things they want. I don't want to make them feel guilty for having a better life than the many less fortunate children in the world. At the same time, I do want them to know that not everyone in the world enjoys the same level of comfort and security as they do. I want them to appreciate all they have and be grateful for it. And according to Carter, that means setting up habits in their daily lives that nurture gratitude.

The disappointment of things

Another reason that material abundance may lead to a state of disappointment rather than gratitude is that material things, by their very nature, are destined to disappoint. They wear out. They break. They turn out not to be as exciting as they seemed in the ads. They fall out of fashion. Eventually the object ends up forgotten at the back of a drawer, left in a charity donation box, or dumped on a landfill.

For adults as well as kids, buying or being given a desirable new possession often brings a thrilling rush of happiness. That feeling soon begins to fade, until we are

> "Gratefulness is the key to a happy life that we hold in our hands, because if we are not grateful, then no matter how much we have we will not be happy— because we will always want to have something else or something more."
>
> **David Steindl-Rast**

back to feeling the same way we felt before. This process is called "hedonic adaptation." That's a fancy way of saying that we get used to new things in our lives (both good and bad) and return to our old run-of-the-mill level of happiness. When the high of owning a new possession wears off, we may buy something new—or children may beg us to buy it for them—to try and recapture that elated feeling, which then fades. And around and around we go.

Thanks to hedonic adaptation, a life centered on the pursuit of material things is almost destined to lead to disappointment— and disappointment's good friend, lack of gratitude. And if giving material gifts to our children is our primary way of expressing love or rewarding their good behavior, we are inevitably setting them up for disappointment and lack of gratitude. I'm not suggesting that anybody stop shopping and giving gifts. I love splurging on the occasional indulgence; and picking out the ultimate gifts for people is one of my greatest pleasures in life. But I do think we should always strive for balance. There are plenty of other ways to show love and affection—such as smiles, hugs, kind words, and acts of service—and we should use them generously with our children and with the other people in our lives so that we can show our children how much more there is to life than material objects. Research showed that teens who strongly associated material wealth with success and happiness got poorer grades at school than their less materialistic peers and were more depressed and had a more negative outlook on life.

By making gratitude one of the daily habits of our families, we can help to interrupt the crazy-making cycle in which we give kids the things they have been begging for, they are momentarily pleased, and then the pleasure wears off, leaving them begging for something else. When we pause for a moment to think about all we have to be grateful for, we are less likely to feel that we are lacking. We are more likely to be aware of the abundance all around us, which can help take away that desperate aching craving for the next material possession. Research backs this up. Robert Emmons and Michael McCullough found in one of their studies that "grateful individuals place less importance on material goods; they are less likely to judge their own and others' success in terms of possessions accumulated; they are less envious of others; and are more likely to share their possessions with others relative to less grateful persons."

Are you a grateful parent?

When I'm talking to parents about how to help their kids navigate the challenges of childhood and adolescence, I'm forever encouraging them to model the kind of attitudes and actions they would like to see in their kids. "Kids cannot be what they cannot see!" is my mantra, and I think it's especially relevant when it comes to instilling gratitude. Kids soak up everything we do and say. Even the most seemingly mundane moments of our life are really lessons that we're teaching them. If just by living our lives we are leading by example, it makes sense to try and live the kind of life we want our kids to lead. By modeling a grateful attitude and behavior, you will not only be setting yourself up for greater happiness and positivity, you'll also be setting your kids up to become more grateful . . . which in turn will generate a whole lot of happiness and positivity for them. Everybody wins a prize when they play this game.

According to the experts, it's the little things we do and say every day that make all the difference, rather than grand gestures. That means all those times you say "please" and "thank you" to your partner, the stranger who holds open the door for you, the person waiting on your table, your kids' teachers, and so on, you are nurturing the seed of gratitude in your kids.

I'm not saying it will always be easy. There will be days when everything seems to be conspiring against a sunny, grateful attitude. Really, all any of us can do is work with what we have on any given day and do our best. Even Mother Teresa wrote about having dark times. If the modern world's very embodiment of generosity and gratitude had her struggles, you certainly have the right to not get it right all the time! I think the most important thing is to be mindful and gently ask ourselves if we are putting out the kind of grateful energy we would like to see in our kids.

For me the biggest family gratitude battleground is the dinner table. You know that internet meme of the woman slumped in a chair, forehead on her arm, despairing, "Why do they want to eat every single night?" That woman is me. I feel almost resentful of the fact that at the end of a day of work I have to prepare something to put on the table . . . and not just anything, but something tasty that my kids will actually want to eat. And then do it again the next day. And every freaking day after that. Let's just say, I need a lot of validation for my efforts. When my kids say thanks, it just isn't enough to satisfy me. I almost need a marching band. And banners!

When I feel my resentment rising to a crescendo, I laugh and think of my own mother, who, like me, was only satisfied when she was thanked effusively and continuously at the dinner table, as though we were gushing about a Michelin-starred restaurant. She would say relentlessly throughout the meal, "Do you like it?" "Is it nice?" "What would you give it out of ten?" Some nights if I serve a meal it would be polite to describe as average, my daughter, Teyah, will crack me up with one of her brilliantly honest teen-girl reviews in response to my own validation-seeking barrage of "Do you like it?" "Is it nice?" "What would you give it out of ten?"

I guess what I'm saying is that perhaps it is exactly when we find ourselves complaining about the entitlement of young people these days that we would benefit most from pausing to check our own hearts and minds!

Gratitude quiz

Take the gratitude quiz to get an idea of where you are now on the gratefulness scale, and where you would like to be. For each of the following statements, give yourself a score from 1 to 7.

1 = strongly disagree
2 = disagree
3 = slightly disagree
4 = neutral
5 = slightly agree
6 = agree
7 = strongly agree

1. There is so much in my life for which to be thankful—a whole abundance of people and things!
2. If you asked me to write a list of all the things I'm grateful for, you would need to give me a very big notebook.
3. To me the world looks like a place that offers many things for which to be grateful.
4. The people for whom I'm grateful come from many different walks of life.
5. With each passing year, my appreciation deepens for the people, events, and circumstances that have played roles in my life story.
6. Little time passes between my moments of gratitude for the people and things in my life.
7. I am fortunate to have been bestowed many gifts in my life.

8. It's easy to make me feel appreciative.
9. Life itself is something to be thankful for.
10. My thoughts often turn to how my life is a lot easier thanks to other people's efforts.

What your score means

53–70: You see all the gifts that your life and the world have to offer. If you keep modeling this kind of attitude and the grateful actions that go along with it, you will be providing your children with the best possible lessons in how to live gratefully.

46–52: While you feel grateful when things are going well in life, it can be harder to be thankful when the going gets tough, can't it? Spending some time each day to shift your focus from the obstacles and challenges in your life may help you to see more of the positives.

10–45: Right now for you the world seems to offer more burdens than gifts, doesn't it? You are not alone. That is why so many people have come up with exercises to help cultivate gratitude. The best part? They work! My hope is that in the practical advice that follows you will find some hints and tips that are a good fit for you.

Tips, hints, and practical ideas for being a grateful parent

If you find that you are struggling to live a grateful life, or you want to make sure you keep your gratitude muscle healthy and strong, here are some practical exercises and tips to try.

The gratitude journal

It can be all too easy to focus on the problems and challenges we have in life, at the expense of noticing the good stuff. For the next week, each night before you go to sleep, take 10 minutes or so to reflect on your day and recall three things that went well. Write these down in a journal. Next to each of the three things, write why it happened. It doesn't matter what form your journal takes. Scribble in an old exercise book, type into your computer or smartphone, do calligraphy with an ink-dipped quill in a leather-bound notebook—just be sure to write it down! The reason I stress this is that when you turn your thoughts into written words, you have a greater chance of success, because writing helps you to organize and integrate your thoughts and put them in context.

Keeping a gratitude journal will make you more perceptive of the joys all around you. If you have been taking anything for granted, you will now be more likely to see its value. The practice can have its most powerful benefits on those days day when you feel as though everything's wrong and that you can't possibly find anything good to write down. An amazing thing happens: you find that you do have three things to be thankful for, no matter how basic and simple those things might be—the oxygen you are breathing into your lungs, the roof above your head, the earth beneath your feet. You can go back and read previous entries to see all that you have been thankful for in the past, which can be especially helpful when you're feeling less than grateful for what life is serving up for you right now. Just when you need it most, journaling proves that you have an abundance of gifts.

Focus on the good in your children

Because it's so important to model gratitude to our children, I especially want to include some tips about showing gratitude *for* our children...

There is a lot of pressure these days on kids to excel—to do well at school, have a special talent, be great at sports, be popular, and the list goes on. As parents there is also pressure on us to provide the support our children need in order for them to excel. The days can become a blur of activities that all seem to be focused on helping our children fulfill their greatest potential—checking homework, coaching them to develop study skills, hiring tutors, ferrying them to their sports, music lessons, theater groups, community volunteer jobs, and more.

In this whirlwind of activities, it's important to make sure that we're making our kids feel loved and supported, rather than only adding to the pressures they feel. Certainly we need to do what we can to help our kids develop the skills they will need to succeed as adults. But we also need to let them know—often and openly and joyously—that while they have a lot of growing up to do, they are also *fine just how they are right now* and we're grateful they are in our lives.

Our children need to know how much we appreciate them and that our love isn't conditional on them coming top of their class, making it onto the team, being the most popular student in their year, or getting the leading role in the school play. If we show our gratitude and appreciation for who they are right now, we are setting them up with the foundation to grow into grateful, appreciative adults.

As with all forms of expressing gratitude, it works best if we are specific. Find ways to tell your kids how much you appreciate them for their unique qualities. Maybe it's their amazing sense of humor, their smile, their compassion for animals, the fact that they helped your elderly neighbor prune his rosebush the other day, that you love the way their hair smells (okay, maybe that's just me—I love to sniff my children!), or that they give the *best* hugs. Whatever it is you appreciate about your children, let them know! After all, you can't really expect them to be grateful if they don't know how grateful *you* are.

A lot of parents wonder whether it's a good idea to thank their kids for doing chores that they should simply be expected to do, such as cleaning their rooms or helping clean up after dinner. Psychologist Jeffrey Froh says yes, "because it's a great way to reinforce positive behavior." The way I look at it, if we expect our children to show appreciation and gratitude, we need to show ours to everyone, and that includes them.

One reason the gratitude journal is so effective is it makes us focus on what's positive in our life. We can apply the same principle to cultivating a more grateful attitude toward our children. If you focus only on what your kids are doing wrong, it's going to be super difficult to express to them genuine gratitude and appreciation. Instead of cataloging all the wrongs, try writing down a list of your children's good qualities and the things they are doing right. Then write down why you are grateful for those things.

Focusing on the good in children works effectively in schools, too. Teacher educator Kerry Howells, of the University of Tasmania, encourages teachers to try a gratitude practice in which they work on an area of resentment they have. One teacher who tried the exercise worked at changing her negative outlook about a student, a girl who all the teachers in the school found to be troublesome. The teacher made an effort to think about the student's good aspects, and then thanked her. That was the spark the student needed. She started to "become more involved, more connected, she started to do more in class, and many of the other teachers started to notice changes, just from that one teacher working with that one student," says Howells.

The gratitude visit

This exercise requires you to make a pretty significant commitment and also to make yourself a bit vulnerable. For those who are up to the challenge, it is truly worth it. This exercise is the result of decades of research by positive psychologist Martin Seligman. He found that this practice made people significantly happier even up to a month after they did it.

First you need to think of a person you never properly thanked for doing or saying something years ago that changed your life for the better. It needs to be someone who is still alive and whom you could visit next week. That last bit is a dead giveaway. Yes, that's right, I'm going to ask you to visit that person. But before you jump in the car or book a plane ticket, you need to write a letter expressing your gratitude. The letter should be around 300 words long. In it you should say specifically what the person did or said, how the words or actions influenced your life, where you are at in your life now, and how often you recall this person's words or actions. Contact the person and arrange a meeting, but don't mention the purpose of your visit. Then give him or her a surprise by turning up and reading out the letter in person.

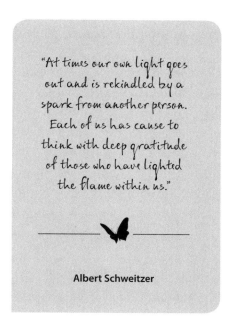

"At times our own light goes out and is rekindled by a spark from another person. Each of us has cause to think with deep gratitude of those who have lighted the flame within us."

Albert Schweitzer

I can almost feel some of you cringing! If the idea of meeting the person face-to-face is all too much to contemplate, or logistically it's just impossible, psychology professor and happiness researcher Sonja Lyubomirsky gives you an out. She says that the act of writing a gratitude letter can lead to greater happiness, even if you don't deliver it.

Can children be taught gratitude?

Chances are there is at least one person in your life who just seems to be naturally grateful—someone who focuses more on what they are thankful for than on the negatives in their life, who gives thanks freely and joyously. It feels pretty good being around that person, doesn't it? You probably notice yourself and everyone in the room gravitating toward him or her. That's because when people live gratefully, their happiness and generosity flow out and touch everyone and everything around them—and who doesn't want to get close to that?

The good news is that our children don't need to be born with a particular personality to become grateful. Because a grateful outlook is something that is learned and developed, there is actually a lot we can do to help foster it in our children.

The tweens and teens I present to in schools prove this to me over and over again. Sometimes when I get to a school, teachers tell me they face a daily struggle to get through to the girls I am about to work with, because they can seem cynical and unappreciative. What I've learned over the years is that the way to break through to these girls is to model love and gratitude by openly expressing how talented, smart, and beautiful I think they are, and how grateful I am for the chance to meet them and share my stories with them.

What I'm doing is giving them permission to share their own love and gratitude for their friends, parents, sisters and brothers, teachers, and all the other good things in their lives. The girls instinctively know that something special is happening: they are in a safe environment in which everyone can share their feelings and vulnerabilities. They know they won't be mocked by their peers (or by adults in their lives, for that matter), and this leads to extraordinary results. Girls line up at the end of a presentation to give me the warmest, most genuine hugs imaginable. I am deluged with incredible letters, emails, and public declarations of undying love and gratitude—sometimes even years after a presentation. Teachers are quite often moved to tears because they've never seen their girls like this. It's a matter of opening the floodgates, and out flows gratitude and generosity that may have been until then deeply hidden from their family, teachers, and even friends.

The reason such transformation is possible is that it innately makes sense and feels good when we show gratitude. It's not something children need to force themselves to do (and certainly not something *we* can force them to do!). If we show kids how to live gratefully and let them know that it's okay to express gratitude, it won't be a chore to them, because it feels so good and so natural.

Gratitude researcher Robert Emmons would agree. He believes that thankfulness comes more naturally for children than it does for adults, because "as we get older, the give and take of life is driven by expectations around tit-for-tat reciprocity. Kids have a natural affinity to gratitude. They often teach parents as much or more about gratitude than the other way around."

Some other researchers, led by Jeffrey Froh, have shown just how quickly children over the age of 8 can grasp the idea of thankfulness. For only half an hour every day for a week, they taught a group of schoolchildren aged 8 to 11 a gratitude curriculum that looked at what it means for someone to take the time and effort to do something that is beneficial to us and that we value. When the children were surveyed at the end of the course, they were found to be substantially more grateful in thought and feeling. As part of the study, members of the parents and teachers association came to give a special presentation to the school after the course; the students who had received the gratitude classes wrote a staggering 80 percent more thank-you notes to the parents and teachers association than the rest of the school did.

After that the researchers taught the same curriculum to another group of students spaced out over a period of five weeks, with one lesson per week. These kids became more grateful and more positive than their peers as time went on. And anyone who thinks that the effort of teaching a child about gratitude is wasted because it won't stick should think again: it turned out that the gratitude gap between the kids who were taught the curriculum and those who weren't was widest *five months* after the course finished.

Every day in my work I see the difference that modeling gratitude can have on young people. The schools where teachers demonstrate gratitude toward me at the end of my workshop by giving me flowers, a card, or a thank-you speech are the schools where students tend to be more thankful, presumably as a result of the culture that the teachers have created. I'm always really astonished and delighted when teachers give me a thank-you gift or speech. After all, they don't have to, as I have been paid to present to the students. Often the teachers are so moved they have tears in their eyes, so I know their gratitude is genuine. And the effect on the students is powerful; the girls tend to be profoundly touched by the gesture of thanks, and there is a chorus of "Awwww!" around the room.

I also give the school a thank-you gift at the end of every workshop, but I give it on behalf of the girls, to really get them involved in the practice of gratitude. I will present the gift to their teacher, first saying something like, "Today has been completely remarkable and amazing. Not all girls get to have this opportunity, and your school thought highly enough of you to want you to have this experience. I know you must be incredibly grateful for that, because I certainly am, so on behalf of you girls, I want to present this to your teacher." The girls love being included in the loop of gratitude, and they always join in giving three cheers for the teacher. Knowing how hard teachers work, this is always a beautiful moment to me.

A quick note about how *not* to teach gratitude

Resilience, not reflex

When you're juggling about 50 million different tasks and trying to keep everybody fed, cleaned, clothed, and delivered safely to school, I admit it can be hard to come up with a logical, reasoned response to kids' whiny ungrateful comments. What I'm about to tell you is something I'm sure you already know: the shortest route to you wanting to tear your hair out and scream is to tell an ungrateful child to feel grateful for something. Yes, we need to teach children from a very early age to say please and thank you, even when they're too young to quite understand what they're saying. But it's counterproductive to try and force kids to *feel* something they're not feeling.

Children need to develop a meaningful, genuine sense of gratitude over time; we can't impose it upon them. There is no point nagging. And though heaven knows we've all thought it sometimes, there is no point in dragging out the old "Think about all the children starving in other countries" line. It's a short cut to guilt and resentment, not genuine gratitude. The last thing we want is to create robots who express gratitude without really feeling it. Once children are old enough to understand the concept of giving and thankfulness, it's time to give them the chance to think about it and really mean it when they say thanks.

A far less hair-pully-outy approach is to make gratitude a daily family habit so that over time it becomes a natural part of our children's makeup. We are more help to our kids when we show gratitude to others, give our children fun opportunities to express gratitude (tips are coming up next), and prompt them to think about the good things they have and where those things came from. Our job is not to force our kids to be grateful. It's to be there to help them find their own way to a place of genuine thankfulness.

You probably have days when you feel angry or miserable, envious or frustrated, and less than thankful for what you're dealing with right at that moment. Kids might not have adult problems such as a mortgage or rent to pay, a hellish boss, or relationship problems, but they do also have days when it's harder for them to feel thankful. Days when they feel sad, angry, disappointed, envious, lacking. I think it's important not to squelch the very real emotions our children have, even the negative ones. All emotions are valid, and children need to know that it's okay to feel them.

If we encourage children to block negative emotions out and simply replace them with rote gratitude, we are only asking for those negative emotions to fester, gain strength, and leak out in some other way. The path to genuine gratitude and happiness is through genuine emotion, so encourage your kids to feel and acknowledge all their emotions, and talk openly about your children's emotions with them. This helps kids develop their emotional literacy, and it also opens up the possibility for them to move forward into a more positive feeling. When we work through our negative feelings, we have the opportunity to see all the things in our lives that we are grateful for.

So raising grateful children is not about minimizing their negative feelings, or pretending that their disappointments don't hurt or they aren't facing real obstacles. It's not about creating Stepford children who see only the good in everything and are happy 100 percent of the time. It's about showing our children by our own example that we can be sad or hurt yet still be grateful for what's good in our lives. After all, if we put off giving thanks until everything was going well and we had everything we wanted, we'd all be a giant pack of ingrates, wouldn't we? Life will always be a mixed bag of joy, achievement, success, and getting what we want—and sadness, loss, challenges, and failure. So what children really need to develop is not a gratitude reflex but true resilience. When we don't get what we want, resilience allows us to see the good or the opportunity in the bad, and pick ourselves up and try again another day.

When a gift disappoints

What parent has not experienced that cringe-inducing moment when their child receives a gift from someone and either won't say thanks or says it through gritted teeth with a tortured face? We do need to acknowledge that sometimes our children will receive gifts that they won't be that impressed by or that actually make them feel upset. Before being too hard on our kids for acting ungraciously, recall how you felt the last time you received a gift that made you feel

"When we give cheerfully and accept gratefully, everyone is blessed."

Maya Angelou

upset, irritated, or underwhelmed. No doubt you were able to cover up your feelings better, but the feelings are the same, and they're real. Usually there is no malice or lack of care behind a gift, but sometimes it does seem that the person doesn't really know you or is in fact sending a passive-aggressive message: "I have to give you a gift, but I'm going to make it meagre or inappropriate." This has nothing to do with the amount of money spent. Some of the best gifts can cost nothing in monetary terms, and even an expensive gift can be upsetting if the person gives it with little thought or purely because he or she feels obliged.

What do we teach our children to do when they receive a gift that, for whatever reason, doesn't feel right? Naturally we teach them to politely thank the person who gave them the gift. Those thankyous oil the wheels of social interaction, and it is important that children know they need to say thanks. But what about our children's feelings of resentment or sadness? Rather than lecture them about how little other children have and how good their life is and how grateful they should be, give them some space to feel disappointed. And when they're ready to talk, talk.

When a gift is not a gift

Another reason it's not a good idea to encourage children to fake gratitude no matter how they feel is that it's important for their safety and happiness throughout life that they learn how to retain appropriate boundaries with other people. They need to learn when to be truly thankful and when it's okay to acknowledge that someone's behavior is affecting them negatively. In rare circumstances, gifts are given not out of wholehearted generosity but out of a darker impulse, such as the urge to control or manipulate.

Amie M. Gordon, Ph.D., warns against "focusing on feeling grateful for someone or something who isn't worthy. If you are in a bad relationship with someone who is emotionally or physically abusing you—or who just can't make you happy—gratitude may be the wrong choice." Automatically adopting a grateful attitude can make you stay "when you should be finding a way to get out of an unhealthy situation. Account for the entire relationship, not just the good parts!" I think this is great to remember when your kids start forming friendships at school and begin dating.

Gordon also cautions us not to use gratitude to avoid serious problems. One thing that's wonderful about having a grateful attitude is that it focuses our minds on the positives rather than the annoyances of life. But it's important to learn to distinguish annoyances from real problems that need to be resolved. "In cases like these, a negative emotion like anger may actually be more constructive," she says. There are many things that we cannot be grateful for, such as violence, unfaithfulness, betrayal, and exploitation, according to one of the most respected thinkers on gratitude, Brother David Steindl-Rast. But when we are facing problems such as these, "this may be an opportunity to learn, to grow, or to stand up and be counted and protest against a situation."

We all hope our kids won't have to deal with serious problems, but no matter how well we protect them while they are children, as adults they need to be able to deal with all that life may throw at them.

Tips, hints, and practical ideas for raising a grateful child

Following is a wide selection of ideas for nurturing children's gratitude, recommended by experts and by ordinary parents. I want to thank all of the psychologists and sociologists who are devoting their careers to unlocking the magic of gratitude. And I want to thank all of the parents out there who have taken the time to blog about this topic and shared inventive, fun, and practical tips that are really effective.

Because every child and every family is different, there is no one-size-fits-all solution, which is why I am giving you so many options. I'm not suggesting you try to do *all* of these things; I offer them up so that you can pick and choose, and experiment until you find the daily gratitude rituals that work best for you and your family.

Encourage your children to express their gratitude in whatever way works best for them. Maybe the gratitude switch gets turned on for them when they write a poem, a story, or a letter about the people and things they're thankful for; for other children it might be drawing a picture, making a collage, taking photos, keeping a journal, making a scrapbook; or older kids might like to post on Instagram, Twitter, or Facebook. I think we also need to encourage kids to do practical things as well as expressing their gratitude—for example, showing their brother or sister their appreciation by doing one of their chores, or helping to clean up the park where they love playing.

The meaning of giving

As adults, to us it seems obvious that if someone gives us something or does something for us, we should be thankful. But that link might not be so clear to kids, so here are a couple of tips for helping them out:

- **The giving of gifts.** Until they are old enough to work, kids have to rely on grown-ups to give them *everything* they need and want, which can lead to an expectation that people just give them stuff. Once your children are old enough to begin understanding the concepts of giving and thanking, don't just remind them to say thanks. Also explain *why* they should be thankful. Talk to them about what generosity is. You can also ask a child to consider the thought behind a gift they've received. What does the gift mean to your child? What did the act of giving mean to the person who gave it?

- **The giving of time and effort.** When your kids are old enough, get them involved in jobs around the house that are appropriate to their age—preparing food, setting the table, cleaning up after meals, looking after pets, helping with laundry and gardening.

When children start doing household chores, they learn to not take your efforts for granted. It also helps them to understand that when someone does something for them, it involves time and effort. Once children realize

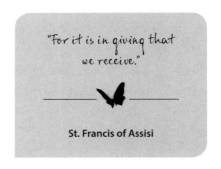

"For it is in giving that we receive."

St. Francis of Assisi

44

this, gratitude is the natural next step. Don't forget to thank your kids sincerely for their contributions around the house! You will be leading by example when you show your appreciation.

Speaking the right language

I am a big advocate for Dr. Gary Chapman's idea of love languages, which he introduced in his book *The 5 Love Languages: The Secret to Love that Lasts*, more than 20 years ago. That book was aimed at couples, but since then he's expanded the idea to kids, too, with *The 5 Love Languages of Children*. Chapman believes that the way people communicate love can be broken down into five languages. All five are important and valid, but each of us has one or more primary love languages that we understand and respond to best. By learning the primary love languages of the people who are important to us, we can communicate better with them and build stronger, more rewarding relationships. The five languages are:

1. Words of affirmation
2. Acts of service
3. Receiving gifts
4. Quality time
5. Physical touch

To be most effective when you show gratitude toward someone, you need to do it in a way that the person will understand that's what you're doing. That is where knowing about love languages can be very valuable. When I cook dinner, I would probably save everybody a lot of angst if I made an official announcement as everybody took their seats that one of my primary love languages is acts of service. If someone thanks me by doing something for me in return, it rocks my world. On the other hand, saying thanks once during the meal just doesn't seem to appease me. I've tried to explain to my kids that when they say thanks while their eyes are on their food and their heads are in the trough, I don't really hear it; I only fully recognize someone's gratitude if they say it with eye contact. And if they don't say it a few times during the meal, I think, "Well, they mustn't really like it." (Don't all be banging down my door at once to get a spot at my dinner table!) What makes me feel as though people really enjoyed the meal and are thankful is if they help me clean up afterward or say, "No, no, you sit down, because you cooked."

I remind myself of this gratitude quirk of mine whenever someone complains that they haven't been thanked though I know for a fact that they have been. Sometimes we *are* being thanked—it's just that we can't hear it. There is a disconnect between us, feeling that we haven't been thanked, and the other person, who's thinking, "But I covered that off. I ticked that box." The reason there's a disconnect is that the person didn't thank us in a way that fits our love language.

I think that talking about love languages is a valuable tool for helping kids build up their emotional literacy and empathy. It's great for them to become aware of their own love languages. And it's great for you as a parent to be aware of their love languages, so you know the best way to validate them in a way that they will really feel that validation. To get things started, you can ask your kids what makes them feel the most loved or happy:

1. "Is it when I say, 'You're a great kid'?" (words of affirmation)
2. "Is it when I surprise you by driving you and your friends to sport?" (acts of service)
3. "Is it when I give you a thoughtful gift?" (receiving gifts)
4. "Is it when the two of us hang out together?" (quality time)
5. "Is it when I hug you?" (physical touch)

There are also great free online tools at www.5lovelanguages.com to help you work out your love languages and your children's.

The parenting approach that I advocate in my work is based on encouraging parents to engage empathically with their children and wholeheartedly show their children love. Parents at my presentations will often counter with, "But my teenager doesn't like it when I'm really affectionate." It is true that teenagers can go through a period in which they feel awkward about receiving words of affection or being hugged—but there are three other love languages you can choose from. Perhaps it's not so much that teens don't like us showing affection, but the *way* in which we're showing affection.

For instance, my teenage daughter, Teyah doesn't like it when I hug her (she jokingly refers to herself as "the Untouchable"). Receiving words of affection also makes her uncomfortable. But she really loves me doing things for her, such as driving her places; she is very grateful for such acts of service. She also appreciates it when I spend time with her, just hanging out and reading, so another of her love languages is quality time. I can see that there are ways to show I love and value her that don't make her feel uncomfortable. I hope that by trying to communicate in Teyah's love language I am also doing some good modeling: if I show that I'm willing to communicate in the way that's most meaningful to her, perhaps she will be more inclined to do the same thing in her interactions with other people.

These are good skills to teach kids early, as they lay the groundwork not only for stronger friendships and personal relationships throughout life but also for career success. One of the most important skills a leader needs is the ability to motivate others by showing gratitude for outstanding performance. This isn't about people pleasing—indiscriminately thanking staff and other colleagues regardless of whether or not their efforts deserve to be rewarded, just so they like you. I don't think there is a place in business for the kind of popularity contests we are all familiar with from high school. I have a team of 10 people, five of whom I directly manage. I expect great work from them—and I don't make any apologies for that, because if you want to be really good at what you do and be a leader, you have to set high standards. And for that reason, when I do thank and praise my team members for their work, they know they have performed exceptionally.

When my team have met or exceeded the targets I've set for them, I show my gratitude using their primary love languages. It will mean the world to one presenter if I publicly acknowledge her outstanding work on Facebook. For another staff member, if I did that she would hit "like" but it wouldn't really rock her as much as if I offered to take her to lunch and spend time with her. When I thank my team, I try to make sure I'm thanking them not in the way that's the easiest or most efficient for me but in the way that they can actually hear the thanks. It's good business practice, but more important, it feels right.

Strengthening the bond

When you express gratitude, you are reaching out to the giver to strengthen a social bond. If you then receive no signal back—no smile or "You're welcome—how do you feel? A bit empty? At the very least, an opportunity to create an even stronger bond has been lost.

That is why I always try to reflect gratitude back to the person who expressed it. This is vital with young people, because they are still getting the hang of giving, receiving, and gratitude. No matter how busy I am or how many emails and letters I receive from kids who have attended my workshops, I send a personal reply of thanks to each one, telling them how much their words meant to me. I know that could be the reward they need to continue to act with gratitude. If I instead just thought "That's nice" and didn't bother replying, those children might think, "Well, what was the point in thanking her?" or, worse, "What's the point in thanking anybody?"

Imagine that when our children thank us, it's as if they're reaching out their hands to take ours. If we don't acknowledge their gesture, it can seem as though we are choosing not to take their hands. Strengthen your bond by acknowledging that you've heard and appreciate your kids' gratitude—a simple smile, hug, or "You're welcome" is all it takes.

Holidays, birthdays, and other big days

Special days such as Christmas and birthdays have the potential to be gratitude nightmares for families. By sundown a day that was supposed to be all about celebration, giving, and gratefully receiving has sometimes ended up being more about tears and resentment. We attach so much meaning to birthdays and holidays, as though all our love must be expressed on these few days of the year. It's almost a setup for disappointment, because while material gifts can be delightful symbols of affection, they can never truly stand in for love.

It's the love, respect, and appreciation that we communicate on the ordinary days that really count. Every day we have the opportunity to see all the wonderful things and people we have in our lives. Imagine how much richer and joyful our lives can be if we show our appreciation and gratitude every day, rather than trying to pour it all into a couple of days a year.

As a young person, I blew some special days because I was so stressed and preoccupied with the idea that everything needed to be perfect, like the jolly scenes that exist only on greeting cards or in ads around the holidays. So when it came to my wedding day, I made a point not to focus on making sure that every little detail was perfect but on being thankful for everything I had. It was an outdoor ceremony, and it was a very windy day. You know something's really up when even the chauffeur driving you to your ceremony has an opinion: he was asking what I was going to do now that the wind had turned my wedding day into a disaster. But I said everything was going to be okay, because I loved my husband-to-be, and I knew the little details would all work themselves out. And they did! I made a point of smiling and making eye contact with everyone that day, and not worrying about things such as my lipstick. And in the photos, I look radiant, because on this joy-filled day I was calm. I've since divorced, but I have a positive relationship with my ex and his new wife, which I'm also very grateful for.

Christmas, birthdays, Mother's Day, Father's Day, Thanksgiving—none of these days will ever go 100 percent according to plan. They will never be perfect. And you know what? Once we accept that, it becomes a whole lot easier to relax and let the genuine love, gratitude, and goodwill flow.

The big celebrations and holidays every year actually provide a bounty of teachable moments. The year I had my Christmas epiphany that led to the book you're now reading, as I stepped on to the plane with my daughter for our trip to the USA, I realized this was a chance for me to try to help her grasp how thankful we both should be for this adventure. I asked her to join me in using the trip as an opportunity to show our gratitude by going out of our way to be kind to others and by exploring the nature of giving thanks.

Our first stop was Texas, where we visited Thanks-Giving Square in Dallas, which has a park, chapel, and museum. I loved the fact that right in the middle of a bustling city was this quiet, light-filled sanctuary established to inspire visitors to think about all they have and all they've been given, and to reflect differently upon obstacles they have faced and see the lessons in those darker moments. I was particularly touched by some of the children's artwork, which reflected the things for which they were thankful.

Teyah and I both wrote notes to add to those left at the Thanksgiving Chapel, reflecting on what I was most grateful for: "I am thankful for the amazing people I get to do life with, and for work which makes my heart dance."

When we moved on to New York, my daughter and I were powerfully moved by the notes and gifts of thanks that are still being left daily for the brave men and women who stepped up during the dark days after September 11. Sometimes when I watch the news I

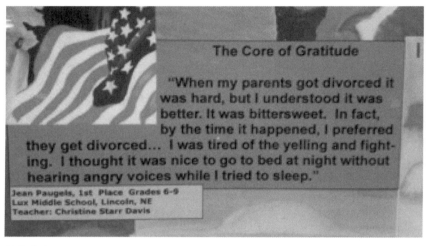

The Core of Gratitude

"When my parents got divorced it was hard, but I understood it was better. It was bittersweet. In fact, by the time it happened, I preferred they get divorced... I was tired of the yelling and fighting. I thought it was nice to go to bed at night without hearing angry voices while I tried to sleep."

Jean Paugels, 1st Place Grades 6-9
Lux Middle School, Lincoln, NE
Teacher: Christine Starr Davis

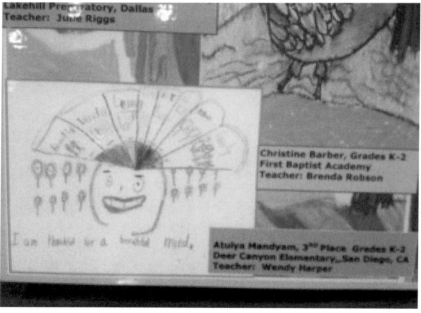

Lakehill Preparatory, Dallas
Teacher: Julie Riggs

Christine Barber, Grades K-2
First Baptist Academy
Teacher: Brenda Robson

I am thankful for a beautiful mind.

Atulya Handyam, 3RD Place Grades K-2
Deer Canyon Elementary, San Diego, CA
Teacher: Wendy Harper

"I am thankful for a beautiful mind."

despair at humanity. Other times, such as when we walked through St Paul's Chapel, directly opposite Ground Zero, I think we humans are amazing. The church remained untouched and became a refuge for rescuers, who slept there in order to maximize the time they spent at their salvage efforts. It's said that 30,000 people from all over the world arrived at the site to assist. As an example, by the end of the first week, 1,000 iron workers from across North America had arrived to help. Inside this place where rescuers had sought shelter, I cried because I was so touched by all the site represents about kindness and connection. Teyah and I added our notes of thanks to the hundreds being left throughout the church.

Here are some other ideas for bringing the spirit of gratitude into special days:

- **Giving as well as receiving.** Get kids involved from an early age in the act of giving, not just receiving. Even when they are very little they can help you select gifts for other people, make their own cards or handicrafts to give, and help you wrap and hand out gifts. Mother's Day and Father's Day are especially good opportunities to get kids actively involved in gift giving—mothers getting kids to make something for dads, and dads getting kids to make something for mothers. The internet is bursting with brilliant age-appropriate craft ideas for Mother's and Father's Day that parents can help their kids do. My daughter once made me a "Jar of Smiles." She got an old glass jar and filled it with fun pictures of us together, some of those funny fake teeth, and strips of paper on which she'd written favorite quotes from inspiring women and little memories she had that she knew would make me happy. I *love* this gift, and it still has pride of place on my dressing table.

- **Christmas love letters.** A mother named Linda Evangelist who hated shopping started a tradition in her family in which they did not exchange presents on Christmas Day but wrote letters listing 25 things they loved about each other. It's become a treasured tradition for many families across the globe since author and journalist Richard Louv wrote about it. I don't think you necessarily have to forgo gifts to do this. (Unlike Linda Evangelist, I *love* buying presents!) And if your kids are very young, you might need to simplify the exercise so everyone can take part.

- **Christmas gratitude calendar.** Christmas can seem like a relentlessly materialistic season, with decorations appearing in stores earlier every year and a barrage of ads everywhere you look. One antidote is to make a gratitude calendar, similar to an Advent calendar. For each of the 24 days leading up to Christmas, an Advent calendar has a little door for kids to open to reveal a message, a toy, or a chocolate. The gratitude calendar has 24 empty pockets. Each day, kids take a small piece of paper, write on it something they're grateful for, and slip it in the pocket. It could be a lot of fun to spend time on Christmas Day reading through all the things everyone's grateful for.

- **A birthday of giving.** I once met a wonderful girl who decided that for her 14th birthday she would ask all the guests at her party not to bring presents for her but presents for dogs. They brought beautifully wrapped dog toys and treats, which the girl happily opened. Then they went to the local dog shelter and had a lovely time giving the dogs the presents. I would never suggest forcing a child to go without birthday gifts, but if your child expresses an interest in turning a birthday into an opportunity to give to a cause, this is a fantastic way to nurture his or her generosity. Only when we understand what it means to give can we fully grasp what it means to receive and be grateful.

- **Thank-you notes.** Never underestimate the power of a simple thank-you note. After the sugar high has worn off, involve children in writing thank-you notes for the gifts they received. If they're very young, have them tell you what they want to say, and write it for them. It's also great to get younger kids to draw pictures that convey their thanks.

Gratitude for friends

It can be all too easy to assume that our friends know how thankful we are to have them in our life, and the same is true for kids. When I work with girls in schools, I ask them to write notes to their friends expressing how much those friends mean to them. It has a *huge* impact. Many of the girls cry happy tears when they tell their friends how grateful they are for their friendship, love, and support.

Of course, it is equally important to encourage boys to show their gratitude for friends. When author, educator, and parenting expert Maggie Dent encourages boys to show friends their thankfulness, they will sometimes hug each other and say, "I love you bro!"

When children learn to not take their friendships for granted but to express how much their friends mean to them, their relationships and support networks are strengthened. They know that others care for them and that they mean something to other people.

Daily gratitude rituals

Like any other important values, gratitude is most effectively developed when it is introduced from an early age as a daily habit, so try and make it just a normal part of life.

- **Bedtime.** Try starting a nightly ritual in which you ask your children at bedtime what their "three good things" are—for instance, the things that went well for them that day, the things that make them happy, the things that fill them with love. What a great way to enter the land of nod—happy, and mindful of all the good in life. This is a tried and true technique, developed and tested by Martin Seligman.

- **Dinnertime.** (You didn't think I was done with the dinner table yet, did you?) An alternative to asking your children at bedtime for their three good things is to go around the dinner table every night, with each person naming one or two things for which he or she is grateful. This reminds everyone that, no matter what their day was like, there is much to be thankful for. And for anyone who wants to bring more connection and communication into family life, it can also be a great conversation starter.

- Those of you who say grace are already formally giving thanks at the dinner table, but I want to emphasize that if you don't want to say grace, you do have other options. For food to end up on your table, there are a lot of people to be thankful for: the person who bought and cooked it; the cashier at the supermarket; the person who stocked the supermarket shelves; the driver who drove it to the supermarket; the people who packaged it, who harvested it, who planted the seeds and watered them, and so on...It could be especially meaningful for your family to write your own words of thanks, or you might like to say this line from a song called "Many Hands," written by Jody Kessler:

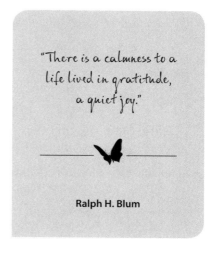

"There is a calmness to a life lived in gratitude, a quiet joy."

Ralph H. Blum

"Let there be gratitude for the many hearts and hands that made this food."

- **The gratitude box.** Some families have a gratitude box. Every day each member of the family writes on a little slip of paper one thing they are thankful for, and then once a week everyone gets together to read them out. This is especially great for busy families who can go for days without all being together in the same place at the same time.

Giving to the community

Developing kindness and generosity toward others by giving to the community helps to grow children's appreciation for all the good things they have. It also helps them learn that everything and everyone is interdependent; no matter how independent we are, we still have other people to thank for much of the good in our lives. Here is a list of ideas to help you find some ways to get kids involved in giving time or resources to the community:

- **Volunteer.** Find out what your children are passionate about and help them find suitable, age-appropriate, and meaningful community work they can do—anything from visiting elderly people at your local nursing home through to helping look after pets at an animal shelter.

- **Help neighbors, friends, and family.** Kids don't have to take up formal volunteer positions to help their community. You probably have some neighbors, friends, or family who need a little help— perhaps they're elderly, disabled, are struggling with their health, or have a new baby. Kids can lighten their burden by helping with gardening, cooking, household chores, and running errands.

- **Look after the local environment.** You and your kids probably have favorite parks or sporting grounds that you go to regularly. By picking up litter when you see it, or getting involved in community clean-up days, you can help kids understand the importance of looking after the environment so that they can enjoy a clean outdoor space and the whole community can benefit.

- **Donate gifts.** Especially at Christmas, many stores take up collections for toys to give to children in struggling families. You may want to help your children select toys or other gifts to purchase to give to less fortunate kids.

- **Donate money.** There are so many good causes seeking our financial support that it can feel overwhelming. As a family, try choosing one or two charities that resonate with you, and give to those.

- **Donate used goods.** A great annual family tradition is to go through all the clothes, toys, and sporting equipment in your closets and donate anything that you no longer wear or use. Try to get your kids involved from an early age in the process, including deciding where the goods should be donated.

Materialism busters

We often have to say no to our children's incessant requests for the latest thing they want us to buy for them. And we all know that simply saying "no" is not so simple—because then come the pleas, the bargaining, the whining.

- **This or that?** Mother Jenn Choi wrote on the Atlantic website about one alternative to just saying "no." Her kids loved Lego and kept on nagging her to buy set after set. She took them to a Lego store where kids can fill a small or large (and more expensive) bucket with bricks. She showed them how, if they took the time and effort and were smart about it, they could fit a lot more pieces into a bucket. She gave them the choice of getting a small bucket's worth, no questions asked, or taking the time and effort to fill a large bucket more strategically. They picked the latter option, and not only had a better appreciation for the mountains of Lego they already had but also became more savvy consumers.

- **Media consumption.** Another way to head off materialism is to help your kids become savvy media consumers. Help them deconstruct all the advertising and marketing messages that encourage them to want more and more products, rather than to feel happy with what they already have. The job of advertisers and marketers is to encourage a sense of dissatisfaction. By questioning the assumptions in ads, you can help your kids see through the gloss.

Physical gratitude prompts
Because gratitude is a habit, physical reminders that kids see or feel every day can be very helpful.

- **Gratitude board.** Have children draw or cut out pictures of things they're grateful for, or write them down on slips of paper.

They can then use these to decorate a gratitude corkboard placed in their bedroom or in a shared part of the house, such as the kitchen, so everybody in the family can take part.

- **Surprise sticky notes.** Give each child a sticky note to write something they're grateful for about another person in the family. Then have them place the sticky note where the person will see it.

- **The pebble of thanks.** Some children respond better to tactile reminders than to visual ones. You can give your child a small, smooth pebble representing all that is good in your child's life. Your child can carry it in a pocket and hold it whenever he or she is having a bad day or feeling disappointed or ungrateful, as a reminder of all there is to be thankful for.

Recognizing everyday heroes

Heroes come in many shapes and sizes. They are not just the people who make the news headlines. They are also ordinary people who do extraordinary things every day to make life better for other people—fire fighters, police, ambulance services, nurses, doctors, teachers, vets, garbage collectors (imagine what the world would be like if garbage collectors didn't turn up for work!). We should be thankful for their efforts, but all too often, these people are overlooked.

- **Think about everyday heroes.** Ask your children to think about who their everyday heroes are, and why. Turning our minds to the everyday people who spend their lives making a difference to our lives reminds us of all we have to be grateful for.

- **Do something for everyday heroes.** One hot, dry summer when property near my home was threatened by fires and the fire fighters had been battling blazes for days on end, I baked a batch of cupcakes and took them down to the station with a note of thanks, and the fire fighters were very grateful for the sweet treats. (And no, I didn't stand there asking, "Do you like them?" "Are they nice?" "What would you give them out of ten?"!) This is the kind of thing that you could get your kids involved in. And you don't need to wait for an emergency to show your gratitude—our police, fire fighters, and ambulance services put themselves on the line every day. Equally, all the other hard-working everyday heroes always deserve our thanks for making the world a better place to live in.

Quiet time

Gratitude researchers note that it's important to have some quiet time alone each day because it gives us time to think about what we're grateful for. All of us have busy lives, and it may be just as hard for kids as it is for us to find time to stop, look around, and appreciate the good things that are happening. Quiet time gives us a chance to pause and see the gifts that are right in front of our faces but that it's so easy to take for granted.

Think about setting some limits on phones and other electronic devices. I'm not suggesting that you cut your kids off from all technology. Actually, I think electronic devices are valuable tools that can enhance children's relationships. It's just as important for kids to text and send messages online as it was for us to spend endless hours writing notes to our best friends and hogging the landline all night. For instance, my son often texts me messages of gratitude and love when he's at his dad's, and they're so incredibly heartwarming that I often take screenshots

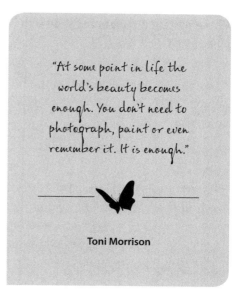

"At some point in life the world's beauty becomes enough. You don't need to photograph, paint or even remember it. It is enough."

Toni Morrison

of them. However, I do think we can all benefit from setting limits so that everyone in the family gets a break in which they have a chance to think back on the day and all the good things it brought.

The antidote to perfectionism

Girls see media images everywhere of what the perfect woman is meant to be—hot, pretty, thin, popular, and nurturing. Boys see what the perfect man is meant to be—good looking, well built, strong, and capable (of everything except cooking, cleaning, or parenting, that is!). Increasingly the images are more and more exaggerated and unachievable—thanks, Photoshop! Too many kids (and adults, for that matter) strive to be perfect and end up with feelings of shame. Perfectionism is all about lack—a feeling of not being good enough the way you are and therefore needing to perfect yourself. When we develop deep gratitude, we know that we are enough and that we have enough. In fact, we know that we have not just enough but an abundance of gifts. Some ideas for growing gratitude and combating perfectionism are:

- Older children can be encouraged to write gratitude letters to their bodies, focusing on all the good things that their bodies do for them.
- Younger children can draw or write about one part of their body that they love.
- You can start a dialogue with kids about this topic and ask them what they appreciate about their bodies.

21-day gratitude challenge

In recent times families have been doing 21-day gratitude challenges and sharing their experiences online. In their research, Robert Emmons and David McCullough found that 21 days is the optimal length for a gratitude challenge, because it doesn't get stale or turn into a burden. If you search online, you will find a host of 21-day plans, with different activities each day. Or the members of your family could take a moment at the same time each day for 21 days to name someone or something for which they are thankful from this list, and briefly explain why:

Day 1:   a friend
Day 2:   a treasured possession
Day 3:   a family member
Day 4:   someone who helped you
Day 5:   a teacher
Day 6:   something in nature that makes you happy
Day 7:   a part of your body that you like
Day 8:   a talent or skill you have
Day 9:   a type of food
Day 10:   a machine, gadget, or type of technology
Day 11:   something good that happened to you
Day 12:   something good that happened to someone else
Day 13:   a song
Day 14:   a color
Day 15:   a book that means something to you
Day 16:   a character in a movie or TV show
           that taught you something
Day 17:   something you successfully learned how to do
Day 18:   a sport or other physical activity
Day 19:   one of the five senses (sight, smell, touch, hearing, taste)
Day 20:   a pet or a type of animal
Day 21:   someone or something that makes you laugh

A special note about teens

While experts have found that when younger children and adults list what they are grateful for, their gratitude and happiness level increases, it can be a different story for teens. Because adolescence is a time of growing independence, it can backfire when we ask them to list the reasons why they are grateful for what others have done for them. You may need to put more emphasis on asking them to think about how grateful they are for themselves and their own accomplishments.

In the end...

There are so many things I am thankful for, I don't think I could ever sit still long enough to list them all. A beautiful home surrounded by trees. A car with awesome satellite navigation (I get lost easily). Amazingly fulfilling work that makes me excited to get out of bed every morning. Delicious food. Delicious fragrances. A resilient and strong body. Beauty. Words. Music. Life itself.

More than anything, though, I am thankful for the people I get to do life with.

Try to imagine the world without the people who give you support and love and compassion. Or a world without all the people you have never even met yet rely on every day—for growing the food that's on your table, for bringing electricity and running water to your home, for helping your family when they're sick, and for all the other million and one things that make life better.

Trying to imagine the world without the people who rely on *your* support, love, and compassion is perhaps even harder to do.

As adults, we've learned that we're all in this together; that no matter how independent we are, we will always need to be connected to other people. Our children are still in the process of working that out. They need time to find the balance between independence and interdependence, and to fully understand what it means when someone does something nice for them. The practical tips in this book can help you support your kids as they learn these things, but most of all, you can help them just by showing them every day what a grateful attitude looks like.

Being a parent is perhaps the ultimate act of giving. We make sacrifices and do everything we can to make sure our children are healthy, safe, happy, and are ready for the future. We don't do it because we expect some kind of payback. We do it for the joy of seeing them grow and learn and gradually reveal all the beautiful qualities that make them unique. We do it for moments that make our hearts burst—like when I went to open my mail and found that my daughter had sent me a letter of love and thanks while she was away on a school retreat, or when my son sends me one of his caring, funny, and affectionate text messages.

Even if our kids tried to pay us back for everything we have done for them, they couldn't—just as we could never pay back all the hours our parents or caregivers put in. And that's okay. We can do much better than trying to pay everyone back. We can grow to understand the real meaning of giving and receiving and thanks. We can lead lives of generosity and thankfulness not just for our families but for everyone who makes our lives better and who gives without expecting anything in return. As Elizabeth Gilbert wrote in *Eat, Pray, Love*:

"In the end, though, maybe we must all give up trying to pay back the people in this world who sustain our lives. In the end, maybe it's wiser to surrender before the miraculous scope of human generosity and to just keep saying thank you, forever and sincerely, for as long as we have voices."

References

page 3   "According to one study from 2012 . . ." See "Gratitude
          in Teens Linked with Being Happier: Study," Huffington
          Post, August 11, 2012, http://www.huffingtonpost.
          com/2012/08/11/gratitude-teens-happier_n_1749118.html.

page 6   "Martin Seligman, known as . . ." See James Baraz and
          Shoshana Alexander, "Grateful Heart, Joyful Heart,"
          Gratefulness.org, http://www.gratefulness.org/readings/
          grateful_joyful7.htm.

          "Two psychologists who are prominent . . ." See Robert A.
          Emmons, Ph.D., *Thanks! How Practicing Gratitude Can Make
          You Happier* (New York: Houghton Mifflin, 2007).

page 7   "more joyful, enthusiastic, interested . . ." Ibid., 31.

          "When schoolchildren in 6th and 7th grade . . ." See Diana
          Kapp, "Raising Children with an Attitude of Gratitude," *The
          Wall Street Journal*, December 23, 2013, http://online.wsj.
          com/news/articles/SB10001424052702303773704579270293660965768.

          "When psychologists analyzed parents' . . ." See Jeffrey
          Froh and Giacomo Bono, "Seven Ways to Foster Gratitude
          in Kids," March 5, 2014, Greater Good, http://greatergood.
          berkeley.edu/article/item/seven_ways_to_foster_gratitude_in_
          kids.

          "In another study . . ." See Diana Kapp, "Raising Children
          with an Attitude of Gratitude," *The Wall Street Journal*,
          December 23, 2013, http://online.wsj.com/news/articles/SB1
          0001424052702303773704579270293660965768.

page 8   "more creative, helpful, charitable . . ." Robert A. Emmons,
          Ph.D., *Thanks! How Practicing Gratitude Can Make You
          Happier* (New York: Houghton Mifflin, 2007), 13.

page 9   "Researchers found that gratitude . . ." See Jeffrey Froh and
          Giacomo Bono, "Seven Ways to Foster Gratitude in Kids,"
          Greater Good, March 5, 2014, http://greatergood.berkeley.
          edu/article/item/seven_ways_to_foster_gratitude_in_kids.

          "And grateful kids aged 14–19 . . ." See Ibid.

page 10   "Psychologist Mindy Ma . . ." See Mindy Ma, Jeffrey L. Kibler, and Kaye Sly, "Gratitude is associated with greater levels of protective factors and lower levels of risks in African American adolescents," *Journal of Adolescence* 36, no. 2 (2013): 983–991.

page 12   "almost as bad as shredding . . ." Dan Ariely, quoted in Jessica Gross, "What Motivates Us at Work? 7 Fascinating Studies that Give Insights," TEDBlog, April 10, 2013.

page 16   "Ingratitude is associated with . . ." Lists are adapted from Robert A. Emmons, Ph.D., *Thanks! How Practicing Gratitude Can Make You Happier* (New York: Houghton Mifflin, 2007).

page 17   "Children may begin to . . ." See Ibid.

page 18   "By 12, children generally . . ." See Charles M. Shelton, Ph.D., *The Gratitude Factor: Enhancing Your Life through Grateful Living* (Mahwah, New Jersey: HiddenSpring, 2010), 127.

"children's comprehension of gratitude . . ." Jeffrey J. Froh and Giacomo Bono, *Making Grateful Kids* (West Conshohocken, Pennsylvania: Templeton Press, 2014), 42.

page 19   "The number of people . . ." See Robert A. Emmons, Ph.D., *Thanks! How Practicing Gratitude Can Make You Happier* (New York: Houghton Mifflin, 2007), 152.

page 20   "Children today are growing up . . ." Jean Twenge, "About *The Narcissism Epidemic*: An FAQ on narcissism," www.narcissismepidemic.com/aboutbook.html.

"handing out ribbons to every child in a race . . ." Karen Brooks, "Constant Over-praising Is Damaging Our Kids," The Butterfly Effect, May 28, 2014, http://enlighteneducation.edublogs.org/2014/05/28/constant-over-praising-is-damaging-our-kids/.

"what we are really doing . . ." Helen McGrath, quoted in Karen Brooks, Ibid.

page 22   "even underprivileged children . . ." Christine Carter, "Dealing with Entitled Kids," Greater Good, May 13, 2013, http://greatergood.berkeley.edu/raising_happiness/category/video/P6.

page 24   "Research showed that teens . . ." See Diana Kapp, "Raising Children with an Attitude of Gratitude," *The Wall Street Journal*, December 23, 2013, http://online.wsj.com/news/articles/SB10001424052702303773704579270293660965768.

71

"grateful individuals place less . . ." Robert A. Emmons and Michael E. McCullough, "Highlights from the Research Project on Gratitude and Thankfulness: Dimensions and Perspectives on Gratitude," www.psy.miami.edu/faculty/mmccullough/Gratitude-Related%20Stuff/highlights_fall_2003.pdf.

page 27   "Gratitude Quiz" The quiz is adapted from Michael E. McCullough, Robert A. Emmons, and Jo-Ann Tsang, "The Grateful Disposition: A Conceptual and Empirical Topography," *Journal of Personality and Social Psychology*, 82 (2002): 112–127.

page 29   "Gratitude journal" See Sonja Lyubomirsky, "How to Practice Gratitude," Gratefulness.org, www.gratefulness.org/readings/practice_gratitude.htm; and Robert A. Emmons, Ph.D., *Thanks! How Practicing Gratitude Can Make You Happier* (New York: Houghton Mifflin, 2007).

page 31   "because it's a great way . . ." Jeffrey Froh, quoted in Ginny Graves, "Teaching Kids Gratitude," *Family Circle*, www.familycircle.com/teen/parenting/discipline/teaching-gratitude/?page=2.

page 32   "become more involved, more connected . . ." Kerry Howells, quoted in Kerry Stewart, "Bringing Back Gratitude to a Secular World," September 4, 2013, www.abc.net.au/radionational/programs/encounter/bringing-back-gratitude-to-a-secular-world/4932066.

           "The gratitude visit" See Maria Popova, "A Simple Exercise to Increase Well-Being and Lower Depression from Martin Seligman, Founding Father of Positive Psychology," Brain Pickings, http://www.brainpickings.org/2014/02/18/martin-seligman-gratitude-visit-three-blessings/.

page 33   "She says that the act of . . ." See Sonja Lyubomirsky, "How to Practice Gratitude," Gratefulness.org, www.gratefulness.org/readings/practice_gratitude.htm.

page 35   "as we get older . . ." Robert Emmons, quoted in Diana Kapp, "Raising Children with an Attitude of Gratitude," *The Wall Street Journal*, December 23, 2013, http://online.wsj.com/news/articles/SB10001424052702303773704579270293660965768.

"Some other researchers, led by Jeffrey Froh . . ." See Emily
Campbell, "Grateful Schools, Happy Schools," Greater Good,
November 18, 2013, http://greatergood.berkeley.edu/article/
item/grateful_schools_happy_schools.

page 42   "focusing on feeling grateful . . ." Amie M. Gordon, "Five
Ways Giving Thanks Can Backfire," Greater Good, April 29,
2013, http://greatergood.berkeley.edu/article/item/five_ways_
giving_thanks_can_backfire.

"In cases like these . . ." Ibid.

"this may be an opportunity . . ." David Steindl-Rast, quoted
in Kerry Stewart, "Bringing Back Gratitude to a Secular
World," September 4, 2013, www.abc.net.au/radionational/
programs/encounter/bringing-back-gratitude-to-a-secular-
world/4932066.

page 45   "The five languages are . . ." See Gary Chapman, The 5 Love
Languages: The Secret to Love that Lasts (Chicago: Northfield
Publishers, 2010).

page 54   "Christmas love letters" See Richard Louv, "Christmas Love
Letters," December 17, 2011, http://richardlouv.com/blog/
christmas-love-letters/.

page 55   "Christmas gratitude calendar" See "Some Kids Just Aren't
Thankful," Greater Good, November 25, 2009, http://
greatergood.berkeley.edu/raising_happiness/post/some_kids_
just_arent_thankful.

page 57   "Let there be gratitude . . ." Jody Kessler, "Many Hands,"
Open Way Sanghas and Open Way Mindfulness Center,
www.openway.org/music/many-hands.

page 58   "The gratitude box" See Beth Herman, "Create a Family
Gratitude Box," Famers Almanac, November 21, 2011, http://
farmersalmanac.com/health/2011/11/21/create-a-family-
gratitude-box/.

page 60   "Mother Jenn Choi wrote . . ." See Jenn Choi, "How to Teach
Kids to Be Grateful: Give Them Less," The Atlantic, January 6,
2014, www.theatlantic.com/education/archive/2014/01/how-
to-teach-kids-to-be-grateful-give-them-less/282834/.